Today's step into possibility...

You don't need every answer to move forward—just one clear next step.

Today's step into possibility...

You don't need every answer to move forward—just one clear next step.

date: _____

Today's step into possibility...

_____
_____
_____
_____
_____
_____
_____
_____
_____
_____
_____
_____
_____
_____
_____
_____
_____

You don't need every answer to move forward—just one clear next step.

Today's step into possibility...

date: _____

_____
_____
_____
_____
_____
_____
_____
_____
_____
_____
_____
_____
_____
_____
_____
_____

You don't need every answer to move forward—just one clear next step.

date: _____

Today's step into possibility...

_____
_____
_____
_____
_____
_____
_____
_____
_____
_____
_____
_____
_____
_____
_____
_____

You don't need every answer to move forward—just one clear next step.

Today's step into possibility...

You don't need every answer to move forward—just one clear next step.

date: _____

Today's step into possibility...

_____
_____
_____
_____
_____
_____
_____
_____
_____
_____
_____
_____
_____
_____
_____
_____

You don't need every answer to move forward—just one clear next step.

Today's step into possibility...

You don't need every answer to move forward—just one clear next step.

Today's step into possibility...

You don't need every answer to move forward—just one clear next step.

Today's step into possibility...

You don't need every answer to move forward—just one clear next step.

date: _____

Today's step into possibility...

_____
_____
_____
_____
_____
_____
_____
_____
_____
_____
_____
_____
_____
_____

You don't need every answer to move forward—just one clear next step.

date: _____

Today's step into possibility...

_____

_____

_____

_____

_____

_____

_____

_____

_____

_____

_____

_____

_____

_____

_____

_____

You don't need every answer to move forward—just one clear next step.

date: _____

Today's step into possibility...

_____
_____
_____
_____
_____
_____
_____
_____
_____
_____
_____
_____
_____
_____
_____
_____

You don't need every answer to move forward—just one clear next step.

Today's step into possibility...

You don't need every answer to move forward—just one clear next step.

Today's step into possibility...

You don't need every answer to move forward—just one clear next step.

Today's step into possibility...

You don't need every answer to move forward—just one clear next step.

Today's step into possibility...

_____

_____

_____

_____

_____

_____

_____

_____

_____

_____

_____

_____

_____

_____

You don't need every answer to move forward—just one clear next step.

date: _____

Today's step into possibility...

_____
_____
_____
_____
_____
_____
_____
_____
_____
_____
_____
_____
_____
_____
_____
_____

You don't need every answer to move forward—just one clear next step.

Today's step into possibility...

You don't need every answer to move forward—just one clear next step.

Today's step into possibility...

You don't need every answer to move forward—just one clear next step.

Today's step into possibility...

You don't need every answer to move forward—just one clear next step.

Today's step into possibility...

You don't need every answer to move forward—just one clear next step.

Today's step into possibility...

You don't need every answer to move forward—just one clear next step.

Today's step into possibility...

You don't need every answer to move forward—just one clear next step.

Today's step into possibility...

You don't need every answer to move forward—just one clear next step.

Today's step into possibility...

You don't need every answer to move forward—just one clear next step.

Today's step into possibility...

_____

_____

_____

_____

_____

_____

_____

_____

_____

_____

_____

_____

_____

_____

_____

_____

_____

You don't need every answer to move forward—just one clear next step.

date: _____

Today's step into possibility...

_____
_____
_____
_____
_____
_____
_____
_____
_____
_____
_____
_____
_____
_____
_____

You don't need every answer to move forward—just one clear next step.

date: _____

Today's step into possibility...

_____

_____

_____

_____

_____

_____

_____

_____

_____

_____

_____

_____

_____

You don't need every answer to move forward—just one clear next step.

date: _____

Today's step into possibility...

_____
_____
_____
_____
_____
_____
_____
_____
_____
_____
_____
_____
_____
_____

You don't need every answer to move forward—just one clear next step.

Today's step into possibility...

_____

_____

_____

_____

_____

_____

_____

_____

_____

_____

_____

_____

_____

_____

_____

_____

_____

_____

_____

You don't need every answer to move forward—just one clear next step.

Today's step into possibility...

You don't need every answer to move forward—just one clear next step.

date: _____

Today's step into possibility...

_____

_____

_____

_____

_____

_____

_____

_____

_____

_____

_____

_____

_____

You don't need every answer to move forward—just one clear next step.

Today's step into possibility...

You don't need every answer to move forward—just one clear next step.

Today's step into possibility...

You don't need every answer to move forward—just one clear next step.

Today's step into possibility...

You don't need every answer to move forward—just one clear next step.

Today's step into possibility...

_____

_____

_____

_____

_____

_____

_____

_____

_____

_____

_____

_____

_____

_____

_____

_____

You don't need every answer to move forward—just one clear next step.

Today's step into possibility...

_____
_____
_____
_____
_____
_____
_____
_____
_____
_____
_____
_____
_____
_____
_____

You don't need every answer to move forward—just one clear next step.

date: _____

Today's step into possibility...

_____

_____

_____

_____

_____

_____

_____

_____

_____

_____

_____

_____

_____

_____

You don't need every answer to move forward—just one clear next step.

Today's step into possibility...

date: _____

You don't need every answer to move forward—just one clear next step.

Today's step into possibility...

You don't need every answer to move forward—just one clear next step.

Today's step into possibility...

You don't need every answer to move forward—just one clear next step.

date: _____

Today's step into possibility...

_____
_____
_____
_____
_____
_____
_____
_____
_____
_____
_____
_____
_____
_____
_____
_____
_____

You don't need every answer to move forward—just one clear next step.

Today's step into possibility...

_____

_____

_____

_____

_____

_____

_____

_____

_____

_____

_____

_____

_____

_____

_____

You don't need every answer to move forward—just one clear next step.

Today's step into possibility...

You don't need every answer to move forward—just one clear next step.

Today's step into possibility...

You don't need every answer to move forward—just one clear next step.

Today's step into possibility...

You don't need every answer to move forward—just one clear next step.

Today's step into possibility...

You don't need every answer to move forward—just one clear next step.

Today's step into possibility...

You don't need every answer to move forward—just one clear next step.

Today's step into possibility...

You don't need every answer to move forward—just one clear next step.

date: _____

Today's step into possibility...

_____
_____
_____
_____
_____
_____
_____
_____
_____
_____
_____
_____
_____

You don't need every answer to move forward—just one clear next step.

Today's step into possibility...

_____

_____

_____

_____

_____

_____

_____

_____

_____

_____

_____

_____

_____

_____

_____

_____

_____

You don't need every answer to move forward—just one clear next step.

Today's step into possibility...

You don't need every answer to move forward—just one clear next step.

Today's step into possibility...

date: _____

_____
_____
_____
_____
_____
_____
_____
_____
_____
_____
_____
_____
_____
_____
_____

You don't need every answer to move forward—just one clear next step.

Today's step into possibility...

_____

_____

_____

_____

_____

_____

_____

_____

_____

_____

_____

_____

_____

_____

_____

_____

You don't need every answer to move forward—just one clear next step.

Today's step into possibility...

You don't need every answer to move forward—just one clear next step.

Today's step into possibility...

You don't need every answer to move forward—just one clear next step.

date: _____

Today's step into possibility...

_____
_____
_____
_____
_____
_____
_____
_____
_____
_____
_____
_____
_____
_____

You don't need every answer to move forward—just one clear next step.

date: _____

Today's step into possibility...

_____
_____
_____
_____
_____
_____
_____
_____
_____
_____
_____
_____
_____
_____
_____

You don't need every answer to move forward—just one clear next step.

Today's step into possibility...

You don't need every answer to move forward—just one clear next step.

date: _____

Today's step into possibility...

_____
_____
_____
_____
_____
_____
_____
_____
_____
_____
_____
_____
_____
_____
_____
_____

You don't need every answer to move forward—just one clear next step.

Today's step into possibility...

You don't need every answer to move forward—just one clear next step.

Today's step into possibility...

You don't need every answer to move forward—just one clear next step.

Today's step into possibility...

You don't need every answer to move forward—just one clear next step.

Today's step into possibility...

You don't need every answer to move forward—just one clear next step.

Today's step into possibility...

You don't need every answer to move forward—just one clear next step.

Today's step into possibility...

_____

_____

_____

_____

_____

_____

_____

_____

_____

_____

_____

_____

_____

_____

_____

_____

You don't need every answer to move forward—just one clear next step.

Today's step into possibility...

_____

_____

_____

_____

_____

_____

_____

_____

_____

_____

_____

_____

_____

_____

_____

_____

You don't need every answer to move forward—just one clear next step.

Today's step into possibility...

You don't need every answer to move forward—just one clear next step.

Today's step into possibility...

_____

_____

_____

_____

_____

_____

_____

_____

_____

_____

_____

_____

_____

You don't need every answer to move forward—just one clear next step.

date: _____

Today's step into possibility...

You don't need every answer to move forward—just one clear next step.

Today's step into possibility...

You don't need every answer to move forward—just one clear next step.

Today's step into possibility...

date: _____

_____

_____

_____

_____

_____

_____

_____

_____

_____

_____

_____

_____

_____

_____

_____

You don't need every answer to move forward—just one clear next step.

Today's step into possibility...

You don't need every answer to move forward—just one clear next step.

date: _____

Today's step into possibility...

_____
_____
_____
_____
_____
_____
_____
_____
_____
_____
_____
_____
_____
_____
_____
_____
_____
_____

You don't need every answer to move forward—just one clear next step.

Today's step into possibility...

You don't need every answer to move forward—just one clear next step.

date: _____

Today's step into possibility...

_____
_____
_____
_____
_____
_____
_____
_____
_____
_____
_____
_____
_____
_____

You don't need every answer to move forward—just one clear next step.

Today's step into possibility...

You don't need every answer to move forward—just one clear next step.

date: _____

Today's step into possibility...

_____
_____
_____
_____
_____
_____
_____
_____
_____
_____
_____
_____
_____
_____
_____
_____
_____

You don't need every answer to move forward—just one clear next step.

date: _____

Today's step into possibility...

_____
_____
_____
_____
_____
_____
_____
_____
_____
_____
_____
_____
_____

You don't need every answer to move forward—just one clear next step.

Today's step into possibility...

You don't need every answer to move forward—just one clear next step.

Today's step into possibility...

date: _____

You don't need every answer to move forward—just one clear next step.

date: _____

Today's step into possibility...

_____

_____

_____

_____

_____

_____

_____

_____

_____

_____

_____

_____

_____

_____

_____

You don't need every answer to move forward—just one clear next step.

date: _____

Today's step into possibility...

_____
_____
_____
_____
_____
_____
_____
_____
_____
_____
_____
_____
_____
_____

You don't need every answer to move forward—just one clear next step.

Today's step into possibility...

You don't need every answer to move forward—just one clear next step.

date: _____

Today's step into possibility...

_____

_____

_____

_____

_____

_____

_____

_____

_____

_____

_____

_____

_____

_____

_____

_____

You don't need every answer to move forward—just one clear next step.

Today's step into possibility...

_____

_____

_____

_____

_____

_____

_____

_____

_____

_____

_____

_____

_____

_____

_____

You don't need every answer to move forward—just one clear next step.

Today's step into possibility...

You don't need every answer to move forward—just one clear next step.

date: _____

Today's step into possibility...

_____
_____
_____
_____
_____
_____
_____
_____
_____
_____
_____
_____
_____
_____
_____
_____

You don't need every answer to move forward—just one clear next step.

Today's step into possibility...

_____

_____

_____

_____

_____

_____

_____

_____

_____

_____

_____

_____

_____

_____

You don't need every answer to move forward—just one clear next step.

date: _____

Today's step into possibility...

_____
_____
_____
_____
_____
_____
_____
_____
_____
_____
_____
_____
_____
_____
_____
_____

You don't need every answer to move forward—just one clear next step.

Today's step into possibility...

_____

_____

_____

_____

_____

_____

_____

_____

_____

_____

_____

_____

_____

_____

_____

_____

_____

You don't need every answer to move forward—just one clear next step.

Today's step into possibility...

You don't need every answer to move forward—just one clear next step.

Today's step into possibility...

You don't need every answer to move forward—just one clear next step.

Today's step into possibility...

date: _____

_____

_____

_____

_____

_____

_____

_____

_____

_____

_____

_____

_____

_____

You don't need every answer to move forward—just one clear next step.

date: _____

Today's step into possibility...

_____

_____

_____

_____

_____

_____

_____

_____

_____

_____

_____

_____

_____

_____

_____

You don't need every answer to move forward—just one clear next step.

date: _____

Today's step into possibility...

_____
_____
_____
_____
_____
_____
_____
_____
_____
_____
_____
_____
_____
_____
_____
_____
_____
_____

You don't need every answer to move forward—just one clear next step.

Today's step into possibility...

You don't need every answer to move forward—just one clear next step.

date: _____

Today's step into possibility...

_____

_____

_____

_____

_____

_____

_____

_____

_____

_____

_____

_____

_____

_____

You don't need every answer to move forward—just one clear next step.

Today's step into possibility...

You don't need every answer to move forward—just one clear next step.

date: _____

Today's step into possibility...

_____
_____
_____
_____
_____
_____
_____
_____
_____
_____
_____
_____
_____
_____
_____
_____
_____
_____

You don't need every answer to move forward—just one clear next step.

Today's step into possibility...

You don't need every answer to move forward—just one clear next step.

Today's step into possibility...

You don't need every answer to move forward—just one clear next step.

Today's step into possibility...

You don't need every answer to move forward—just one clear next step.

Today's step into possibility...

You don't need every answer to move forward—just one clear next step.

Today's step into possibility...

You don't need every answer to move forward—just one clear next step.

date: _____

Today's step into possibility...

_____
_____
_____
_____
_____
_____
_____
_____
_____
_____
_____
_____
_____
_____
_____
_____

You don't need every answer to move forward—just one clear next step.

Today's step into possibility...

You don't need every answer to move forward—just one clear next step.

date: _____

Today's step into possibility...

_____
_____
_____
_____
_____
_____
_____
_____
_____
_____
_____
_____
_____
_____
_____

You don't need every answer to move forward—just one clear next step.

Today's step into possibility...

_____

_____

_____

_____

_____

_____

_____

_____

_____

_____

_____

_____

_____

_____

_____

_____

_____

You don't need every answer to move forward—just one clear next step.

Today's step into possibility...

date: _____

You don't need every answer to move forward—just one clear next step.

Today's step into possibility...

You don't need every answer to move forward—just one clear next step.

Today's step into possibility...

You don't need every answer to move forward—just one clear next step.

Today's step into possibility...

date: _____

You don't need every answer to move forward—just one clear next step.

date: _____

Today's step into possibility...

_____
_____
_____
_____
_____
_____
_____
_____
_____
_____
_____
_____
_____
_____
_____
_____
_____
_____
_____

You don't need every answer to move forward—just one clear next step.

Today's step into possibility...

You don't need every answer to move forward—just one clear next step.

date: _____

Today's step into possibility...

_____
_____
_____
_____
_____
_____
_____
_____
_____
_____
_____
_____
_____
_____
_____

You don't need every answer to move forward—just one clear next step.

Today's step into possibility...

You don't need every answer to move forward—just one clear next step.

Today's step into possibility...

You don't need every answer to move forward—just one clear next step.

Today's step into possibility...

You don't need every answer to move forward—just one clear next step.

date: _____

Today's step into possibility...

_____
_____
_____
_____
_____
_____
_____
_____
_____
_____
_____
_____
_____
_____

You don't need every answer to move forward—just one clear next step.

date: _____

Today's step into possibility...

_____
_____
_____
_____
_____
_____
_____
_____
_____
_____
_____
_____
_____

You don't need every answer to move forward—just one clear next step.

Today's step into possibility...

You don't need every answer to move forward—just one clear next step.

Today's step into possibility...

You don't need every answer to move forward—just one clear next step.

date: _____

Today's step into possibility...

_____
_____
_____
_____
_____
_____
_____
_____
_____
_____
_____
_____
_____
_____

You don't need every answer to move forward—just one clear next step.

Today's step into possibility...

You don't need every answer to move forward—just one clear next step.

date: _____

Today's step into possibility...

_____
_____
_____
_____
_____
_____
_____
_____
_____
_____
_____
_____
_____

You don't need every answer to move forward—just one clear next step.

Today's step into possibility...

_____

_____

_____

_____

_____

_____

_____

_____

_____

_____

_____

_____

_____

_____

_____

You don't need every answer to move forward—just one clear next step.

Today's step into possibility...

You don't need every answer to move forward—just one clear next step.

date: _____

Today's step into possibility...

_____
_____
_____
_____
_____
_____
_____
_____
_____
_____
_____
_____
_____

You don't need every answer to move forward—just one clear next step.

Today's step into possibility...

You don't need every answer to move forward—just one clear next step.

Today's step into possibility...

date: _____

_____

_____

_____

_____

_____

_____

_____

_____

_____

_____

_____

_____

_____

You don't need every answer to move forward—just one clear next step.

Today's step into possibility...

You don't need every answer to move forward—just one clear next step.

Today's step into possibility...

You don't need every answer to move forward—just one clear next step.

date: _____

Today's step into possibility...

_____
_____
_____
_____
_____
_____
_____
_____
_____
_____
_____
_____
_____
_____
_____

You don't need every answer to move forward—just one clear next step.

Today's step into possibility...

_____
_____
_____
_____
_____
_____
_____
_____
_____
_____
_____
_____
_____
_____

You don't need every answer to move forward—just one clear next step.

date: _____

Today's step into possibility...

_____

_____

_____

_____

_____

_____

_____

_____

_____

_____

_____

_____

_____

_____

You don't need every answer to move forward—just one clear next step.

Today's step into possibility...

---

date: _____

Today's step into possibility...

You don't need every answer to move forward—just one clear next step.

Today's step into possibility...

You don't need every answer to move forward—just one clear next step.

Today's step into possibility...

You don't need every answer to move forward—just one clear next step.

Today's step into possibility...

You don't need every answer to move forward—just one clear next step.

Today's step into possibility...

You don't need every answer to move forward—just one clear next step.

Today's step into possibility...

_____

_____

_____

_____

_____

_____

_____

_____

_____

_____

_____

_____

_____

_____

You don't need every answer to move forward—just one clear next step.

date: _____

Today's step into possibility...

_____

_____

_____

_____

_____

_____

_____

_____

_____

_____

_____

_____

_____

_____

_____

_____

_____

You don't need every answer to move forward—just one clear next step.

date: _____

Today's step into possibility...

_____
_____
_____
_____
_____
_____
_____
_____
_____
_____
_____
_____
_____
_____
_____
_____

You don't need every answer to move forward—just one clear next step.

Today's step into possibility...

You don't need every answer to move forward—just one clear next step.

Today's step into possibility...

You don't need every answer to move forward—just one clear next step.

Today's step into possibility...

You don't need every answer to move forward—just one clear next step.

Today's step into possibility...

date: _____

You don't need every answer to move forward—just one clear next step.

date: _____

Today's step into possibility...

_____

_____

_____

_____

_____

_____

_____

_____

_____

_____

_____

_____

_____

_____

You don't need every answer to move forward—just one clear next step.

Today's step into possibility...

You don't need every answer to move forward—just one clear next step.

Today's step into possibility...

You don't need every answer to move forward—just one clear next step.

Today's step into possibility...

You don't need every answer to move forward—just one clear next step.

date: _____

Today's step into possibility...

_____
_____
_____
_____
_____
_____
_____
_____
_____
_____
_____
_____
_____
_____
_____

You don't need every answer to move forward—just one clear next step.

Today's step into possibility...

You don't need every answer to move forward—just one clear next step.

Today's step into possibility...

_____

_____

_____

_____

_____

_____

_____

_____

_____

_____

_____

_____

_____

_____

_____

_____

You don't need every answer to move forward—just one clear next step.

Today's step into possibility...

_____

_____

_____

_____

_____

_____

_____

_____

_____

_____

_____

_____

_____

You don't need every answer to move forward—just one clear next step.

Today's step into possibility...

date: _____

_____

_____

_____

_____

_____

_____

_____

_____

_____

_____

_____

_____

_____

_____

You don't need every answer to move forward—just one clear next step.

Today's step into possibility...

You don't need every answer to move forward—just one clear next step.

Today's step into possibility...

You don't need every answer to move forward—just one clear next step.

Today's step into possibility...

_____

_____

_____

_____

_____

_____

_____

_____

_____

_____

_____

_____

_____

_____

You don't need every answer to move forward—just one clear next step.

Today's step into possibility...

You don't need every answer to move forward—just one clear next step.

Today's step into possibility...

date: _____

You don't need every answer to move forward—just one clear next step.

Today's step into possibility...

You don't need every answer to move forward—just one clear next step.

Today's step into possibility...

You don't need every answer to move forward—just one clear next step.

date: _____

Today's step into possibility...

_____
_____
_____
_____
_____
_____
_____
_____
_____
_____
_____
_____

You don't need every answer to move forward—just one clear next step.

Today's step into possibility...

You don't need every answer to move forward—just one clear next step.

Today's step into possibility...

You don't need every answer to move forward—just one clear next step.

Today's step into possibility...

You don't need every answer to move forward—just one clear next step.

Today's step into possibility...

You don't need every answer to move forward—just one clear next step.

Today's step into possibility...

You don't need every answer to move forward—just one clear next step.

Today's step into possibility...

You don't need every answer to move forward—just one clear next step.

Today's step into possibility...

You don't need every answer to move forward—just one clear next step.

Today's step into possibility...

You don't need every answer to move forward—just one clear next step.

date: _____

Today's step into possibility...

_____
_____
_____
_____
_____
_____
_____
_____
_____
_____
_____
_____
_____
_____
_____
_____
_____

You don't need every answer to move forward—just one clear next step.

Today's step into possibility...

_____

_____

_____

_____

_____

_____

_____

_____

_____

_____

_____

_____

_____

You don't need every answer to move forward—just one clear next step.

Today's step into possibility...

date: _____

You don't need every answer to move forward—just one clear next step.

Today's step into possibility...

date: _____

You don't need every answer to move forward—just one clear next step.

Today's step into possibility...

You don't need every answer to move forward—just one clear next step.

date: _____

Today's step into possibility...

_____

_____

_____

_____

_____

_____

_____

_____

_____

_____

_____

_____

_____

_____

You don't need every answer to move forward—just one clear next step.

Today's step into possibility...

You don't need every answer to move forward—just one clear next step.

Today's step into possibility...

You don't need every answer to move forward—just one clear next step.

Today's step into possibility...

date: _____

You don't need every answer to move forward—just one clear next step.

Today's step into possibility...

You don't need every answer to move forward—just one clear next step.

Today's step into possibility...

You don't need every answer to move forward—just one clear next step.

date: _____

Today's step into possibility...

_____
_____
_____
_____
_____
_____
_____
_____
_____
_____
_____
_____
_____
_____

You don't need every answer to move forward—just one clear next step.

Today's step into possibility...

You don't need every answer to move forward—just one clear next step.

Today's step into possibility...

You don't need every answer to move forward—just one clear next step.

Today's step into possibility...

date: _____

You don't need every answer to move forward—just one clear next step.

Today's step into possibility...

date: _____

You don't need every answer to move forward—just one clear next step.

Today's step into possibility...

You don't need every answer to move forward—just one clear next step.

Today's step into possibility...

You don't need every answer to move forward—just one clear next step.

Today's step into possibility...

date: _____

_____

_____

_____

_____

_____

_____

_____

_____

_____

_____

_____

_____

_____

_____

You don't need every answer to move forward—just one clear next step.

Today's step into possibility...

_____
_____
_____
_____
_____
_____
_____
_____
_____
_____
_____
_____
_____

You don't need every answer to move forward—just one clear next step.

Today's step into possibility...

date: _____

_____
_____
_____
_____
_____
_____
_____
_____
_____
_____
_____
_____
_____
_____

You don't need every answer to move forward—just one clear next step.

date: _____

Today's step into possibility...

_____
_____
_____
_____
_____
_____
_____
_____
_____
_____
_____
_____
_____
_____
_____

You don't need every answer to move forward—just one clear next step.

Today's step into possibility...

You don't need every answer to move forward—just one clear next step.

date: _____

Today's step into possibility...

_____
_____
_____
_____
_____
_____
_____
_____
_____
_____
_____
_____
_____
_____

You don't need every answer to move forward—just one clear next step.

Today's step into possibility...

You don't need every answer to move forward—just one clear next step.